KU-725-752

THREE FACES OF BERKELEY
Competing Ideologies in the Wheeler Era, 1899-1919

Henry F. May

Chapters in the History of the
University of California
Number One

Center for Studies in Higher Education and
Institute of Governmental Studies
University of California, Berkeley
1993

©1993 by the Regents of the University of California. All rights reserved.
Printed in the United States of America.

Library of Congress Cataloging-In-Publication Data
May, Henry Farnham, 1915-
  Three faces of Berkeley competing ideologies in the Wheeler era, 1899-1919 / Henry Farnham May.
        p. cm. -- (Chapters in the History of the University of California ; no. 1)
     ISBN 0-87772-342-7
     1. University of california, Berkeley--History--20th century. 2. Wheeler, Benjamin Ide, 1854-1927. 3. University of California, Berkeley--Presidents--Biography. I. Title. II. Series.
LD759.M39 1993
378.794'67--dc20   93-30444
                                                                              CIP

(1993)

1916.

THREE FACES OF BERKELEY
Competing Ideologies in the Wheeler Era, 1899-1919

In honor of the 125th anniversary of the founding of the University of California, the Center for Studies in Higher Education at Berkeley, in cooperation with the Institute of Governmental Studies, takes pleasure in publishing a series of "chapters" in the history of the University. These are designed to illuminate particular problems and periods in the history of U.C., especially its oldest and original campus at Berkeley, and to identify special turning points or features in the "long century" of the University's evolution. Histories are stories meant to be read and enjoyed in their own right, but the editors cannot conceal the hope that readers of these chapters will notice facts and ideas pertinent to the decade that closes our own century and millennium.

Carroll Brentano and
Sheldon Rothblatt, editors

General Campus View, University of California.
BERKELEY.

Campus View

FOREWORD

The following essay by Henry May on the era of President Benjamin Ide Wheeler opens our series of "chapters" in the history of the University of California. The series is a product of the labors of the members of the University History Project sponsored by the Center for Studies in Higher Education. Editors and contributors alike are particularly grateful for the help received from participants in the monthly seminars, which met over a four-year period to discuss the sources and writing of university history. Many speakers and visitors from other states and from abroad have shared with us their knowledge and ideas and have helped teach us how to see our own local history in broader historical perspective. We are especially cognizant of the assistance of William Roberts, University Archivist, and of other members of the Bancroft Library and the Oral History Project. The editorial acumen of Janet Ruyle, Assistant Director of the Center, was invaluable, and we wish to thank her, as well as another member of the Center's staff, Patricia Paulson, for lending a hand so cheerfully.

We owe a special debt to our predecessors. Verne A. Stadtman's *The University of California 1868-1968,* published in 1970, remains the foundation text, and we are pleased that he was able to participate in our meetings. President Emeritus Clark Kerr encouraged us from the start not only by setting the example for a university history project many years ago, but by providing us with his active as well as moral support. President Emeritus David Gardner and two Berkeley chancellors, Ira M. Heyman and Chang-Lin Tien, gave us similar encouragement and financial help. The Department of History on the Berkeley campus through its former chair, Professor Robert Middlekauff, was also a benefactor, and we are grateful for the recognition offered by our history colleagues.

In the last dozen to 15 years, the subject of university history has received extraordinary international attention. Single-authored works are produced yearly, and new specialized journals exist. In a large number of notable instances, the wealth and complexity of source material have led to the fashioning of major collaborative projects. The most ambitious of these is the history of Oxford University, of which five volumes have been published to date (on top of a vast corpus of existing histories), but significant work has also been done on the history of Cambridge, Aberdeen, and Birmingham universities. The Standing Conference of Rectors, Principals, and Vice Chancellors of the European Universities, with headquarters in Geneva, has commissioned four volumes on the history of the university since its medieval origins. At least two centers for encouraging the study of Italian university history exist, one in the form of the International Center for the History of the Universities and Science at Bologna, and another also recently established by the Universities of Trent, Naples and Siena at Trent. A team of scholars at the Hebrew University in Jerusalem is in the beginning stages of a major study of Israel's first university, and in Germany and Sweden, as well as Finland, the study of the history of universities and higher education is well-advanced and supported by publicly funded research councils.

In the United States, private universities such as Harvard and Chicago continue to add to the impressive corpus already available on their historical development, and in 1992 a general history of higher education in Massachusetts appeared. The University of Pittsburgh can also claim a new general history for itself.

Judged by such standards, work on the University of California is less extensive, but several recent achievements

need to be noted. In the history of some of its leading architects and their buildings, we can name the important books by Loren Partridge and Sally Woodbridge. John Heilbron's and Robert Seidel's volumes on the history of the Lawrence Berkeley Laboratory are a major addition to an accessible body of writings on the University of California. Works on the history of crew and the Berkeley Faculty Club are in the offing. As the oldest of the campuses, Berkeley has received more attention than the later campuses, but we are pleased to notice new work on the history of the College of Agriculture on the Davis and Berkeley campuses by Ann Scheuring and on the Irvine campus by Samuel McCulloch.

By these examples, by our own initial efforts, and by the ambitious projects of our colleagues abroad, we hope to stimulate further interest in a subject that is no less than the story of the civilization of modern times as encapsulated in an institution with an ancient pedigree. Universities have become one of society's most central institutions because of a combination of historical outcomes, amongst which can be numbered the evolution of mass higher education and the efflorescence of "big science" and high technology. But universities also retain their ancient prominence in training members of the leading professions and in preparing students for citizenship and leadership in the great democracies.

What may be of special interest to Californians are the long-standing and entangled but successful interrelationships between state, society, and higher education that we hope can continue despite the spectacular changes all have undergone since the University's modest beginnings. Our "chapters" are designed to explicate the complexity of the interdependence. Although California sprang up like a gourd in the night, according to the opinion offered a century ago by the eminent British historian, jurist, and diplomat Lord Bryce, and its university at nearly the same speed, the state's relations to its

University are far greater and more intricate than at any time in the past. Today California is the most heterogeneous of the nation's states. It is also the largest in population and has the greatest number of new immigrants. California has many publics, and each has played and continues to play a significant part in the history of its University. Our authors have tried to reproduce in words and mental (sometimes in actual) pictures the colorful, bewildering, and many-sided character of innumer- able personal and institutional connections.

In his "chapter," Henry May concentrates on the Age of President Wheeler because only then did the University come into its own. Earlier periods were marked by fierce conflicts over the University's public and educational mission and its relationship to state, society, and school. Instability hampered its growth, partisan interests competed for its loyalty, or even subservience. Lacking stability, U.C. was unable to establish a distinct identity within the pantheon of world universities. But by 1910 national recognition and self-confidence had been achieved. "Believing that California's geographical position affords her a remarkable opportunity for the development of originality free from the hampering influences of ancient precedents and prejudices," wrote the youthful editors of the student annual, *The Blue & Gold* for 1915, "this volume aims to record our own pleasures and problems, not only as we see them but also as the social workers of universal experience see them." Here was the self-conscious mix of boosterism and cosmopolitanism that defined the California style and made the state, as May observes, and by association its public university, an exaggeration of American culture itself.

A commonplace of today's historical writing about universi- ties is to remark upon their highly diverse and complex internal characteristics, their "autonomous" disciplines and the absence of a strong core of shared values. These are not the result of accident or willfulness but the outcome of the university's very responsiveness to the astonishing demands upon it by the outside world. According to May, these features are first visible in the Wheeler period. It is from those years that we can date the high internal differentiation typical of the present-day institution. There was not one Berkeley, comments May, but several. Originating in different aims and purposes, they could not be smoothly integrated and harmonized. Even as colorful and indeed as legendary a president as Wheeler could not reconcile the differences. Strong regents and presidents had maintained firm control of the direction of the University since its birth, but before Wheeler left office the changes in academic career values were producing rifts and controversies over the powers of appointment and governance and the influence over academic program.

In a number of critical ways, therefore, the twentieth-century history of the University of California had commenced.

Sheldon Rothblatt

ACKNOWLEDGEMENTS

I want to thank the staff of the Bancroft Library for assistance and for permission to quote manuscript materials. All manuscript collections cited are in that library. I am grateful to the Center for Studies of Higher Education, and especially Carroll Brentano, for many important kinds of assistance. William Roberts, University Archivist, has also been helpful. This essay has benefited from critical readings by Bruce Kuklick, Kenneth M. Stampp, and Laurence Veysey. Finally, since I am a newcomer to this subject, I have depended heavily on the devoted work of many investigators. I am particularly grateful to Verne Stadtman for his excellent short history, with mainly administrative emphasis, *The University of California, 1868-1968* (New York, 1970); and also for his immensely useful compilation of miscellaneous information, *The Centennial Record of the University of California* (Berkeley, 1965), hereafter cited as *Centennial Record*.

Henry F. May

ILLUSTRATIONS

*All figures are courtesy of the University of California, Berkeley,
Archives.*

Benjamin Ide Wheeler

THREE FACES OF BERKELEY
Competing Ideologies in
The Wheeler Era, 1899-1919

In embarking on the academic study of the University of California, I have one doubtful advantage: my long association with the institution and its milieu. I was brought up in Berkeley in the twenties, when much of Benjamin Ide Wheeler's Berkeley was still alive. I was an undergraduate at Berkeley in the thirties and a faculty member from the early fifties. I call this a doubtful advantage because long association has its dangers as well as its advantages. One danger is nostalgia, always a menace to historians. I find, and think others may find, a lot about the University in the Wheeler period rather attractive. Yet there were many limitations and shortcomings, and it is no service to the University to understate these, in dealing with this period or any other. I want equally to avoid the opposite danger, that of judging the past purely in terms of present assumptions, or, still worse, finding the past reprehensible or comical because it is different from the present. I want to try to present Wheeler's University as it was—of course an impossible task, but one worth attempting. I want to do my best to understand how different kinds of people, especially faculty and administration, saw the meaning and purpose of the University of California at a crucial time in the past.

I want especially to look at the history of the University as a part of American cultural history. Berkeley and its University were, after all, part of the United States, the United States of Theodore Roosevelt, William Jennings Bryan, and William James. Berkeley was also a part of the prewar world, a world in which European culture took for granted its own unthreaten-

1

ed hegemony. I have argued elsewhere that America in that period, under its bland and progressive surface, was deeply divided between defenders of the existing official culture and a vigorous, diverse cultural rebellion that would become much larger and more articulate after the war.[1]

Berkeley was also a particular place— a western place. I believe that real cultural innovation in this period and most others did not come from the frontier, as some historians influenced by Frederick Jackson Turner long insisted, but rather from the confident, established centers of American culture, from the regions of Boston, New York, and Chicago. On the frontier, traditional culture was too fragile to be tampered with. The Bay Area was and was not frontier. Traces of its violent and raffish Gold Rush past were still evident, yet most visitors to San Francisco were surprised at the confident, cosmopolitan urbanity they found in the western metropolis. On the whole the Bay Area in the early twentieth century played a culturally conservative role and was comfortable doing so. One can find little in San Francisco of the America of Ezra Pound or Randolph Bourne or the Armory Show. In architecture, theater, music, and food San Francisco aimed at traditional excellence rather than innovation.[2] And in this conservative taste Berkeley was part of its region. This does not necessarily mean that the University was without certain subtle, unheralded kinds of newness.

Long ago, I got the idea of working on cultural division in this period from reading a great speech, delivered in the Greek Theater in 1911 by the Harvard philosopher George Santayana (he would hate to be called that, because he hated Harvard). Santayana, speaking with great brilliance and unique detachment about his partly adopted nation, said that America was a country with two mentalities. One was exemplified by business and commerce and was busy and practical and in some ways innovative. The other, exemplified by American literature, religion, and "the moral emotions," was becalmed and behind the times.

> [T]his division may be found symbolized in American architecture: a neat reproduction of the colonial mansion—with some modern comforts introduced surreptitiously —stands beside the sky-scraper. . . . The one is all aggressive enterprise, the other is all genteel tradition.[3]

Santayana drew his examples from the only America he knew, Cambridge and Boston. He ended by hoping that California, drawing energy somehow from its mountains and forests, would free itself from this dichotomy. He did not realize that the University in which he was speaking was a prime example of this division carried to extremes— the genteel tradition even more genteel than in the East and more on the defensive, its opponents tougher, more confident, and more aggressive.

Yet somehow the two halves of the American mentality managed to coexist here, some thought with remarkable and mysterious success. In 1910 a very lively publicist named Edwin E. Slosson, who could not have read Santayana's statement, included Berkeley in his study of 13 great American universities. In his highly interesting essay on Berkeley he said the following:

> The University of California derives its origin from the union of a New England classical religious college and a Morrill Act school of agriculture and mechanic arts [approximately correct]. It takes after both sides of the house, according to Galton's law. The combination of qualities that are quite diverse and even antagonistic give the institution a unique attractiveness. I know of no other university which cultivates both mechanics and metaphysics with such equal success or which looks so far into space, and, at the same time, comes so close to the lives of the people; or which excavates the tombs of

the Pharaohs and Incas while it is inventing new plants
for the agriculture of the future.[4]

My principal purpose here is to try to understand how, insofar
as this statement was true in 1913, this University had become
so good at making this combination of opposites work.

Why concentrate on the Wheeler period (1899-1919)?
Here, and at many other points throughout this essay, I depend
on a really illuminating book, Laurence Veysey's *The Emergence of the American University.*[5] Looking in surprising
depth at *all* the major American universities, Veysey argues con-
vincingly that in the period 1865 to 1910 a new kind of
institution came into being. The American university, which
then took on most of its present form, was quite unlike either
the British or the German university. Though influenced by
both of these, it was formed by and reflected the culture and
polity in which it grew. In a later essay Veysey makes the
following statement: "The decades between 1870 and 1910 witnessed the only genuine 'academic revolution' yet to be experi-
enced in the United States."[6] This is a strong statement,
especially since Veysey made it in 1973, after living through
both the 1950s and the 1960s. Some of us in Berkeley thought
we were going through revolutions in each of these two very
different decades. Yet I think Veysey's statement is worth
thinking about and may well be true.

In this period, things happened a little later on the West
Coast. Also, there were particular reasons why Berkeley had
been unable to "emerge" as a major university before Wheeler
took over. I don't wish to slight his predecessors. Under
different circumstances, Daniel Coit Gilman (president 1872-75)
might have been a brilliant president of the University of
California, as he was of Johns Hopkins after he left Berkeley.
William T. Reid (1881-85) and Martin Kellogg (1893-99) were
both devoted and talented men who increased the stature and
strengthened the institutional framework of the University.

Despite all the devotion and effort, the University had not become a major institution with a national standing commensurate with the growing wealth and power of the state.

A university, to flourish, needs a combination of stimulus and stability. Stability, before the Wheeler period, had been spectacularly lacking. The main destabilizing force was a long series of violent political attacks carried on in the name of democracy and utility. Such attacks can, of course, come from either the political left or right, and have in the University's history come from both quarters, and even from both at once. In the 30 years before Wheeler came, the most dangerous attacks were part of a popular onslaught against elitism, carried on by Kearneyites, Grangers, and other labor and agrarian groups. Some had wanted to make the University part of the public school system, others to have it directly run by the legislature, still others to force it to teach *only* what they called mechanical arts and sciences. It had fended off these attacks with great difficulty, the most dangerous point coming in the late 1870s when the regents very narrowly managed to establish their absolutely crucial independence.[7] The governmental system of the University had developed into a thoroughly Madisonian system of checks and balances, with power balanced among the legislature, the regents, and the university administration. Neither faculty nor students had yet become major players in the power game, though obviously both had to exist and to be contented enough to stay around. The administrative history of the University can be summarized by a succession of episodes in which one or another of the balanced forces came close to seizing power. Early on it was the legislature, then the regents; in Wheeler's period it was the president; after his fall, the faculty, and in the 1960s briefly, the students.

In the period right before Wheeler, the regents, the necessary mainstay of the university's free existence, had gotten into some bad habits. They constantly interfered directly in the detailed running of the institution, hiring or promoting professors they liked, getting rid of those they did not like, and in general leaving the presidents, some of them very able, little scope and no security. The average duration of the pre-Wheeler presidencies was less than four years.[8]

Wheeler managed to last 20 years—17 of them in complete control of the situation. This fact constitutes much of the importance of his reign. With all its faults, the Wheeler presidency gave the University some time to emerge as a major institution. This is suggested partly by statistics:[9]

	1898-99	1919-20
Students at Berkeley	1,717	9,967
Faculty at Berkeley	105	390

But numbers are only part of the story. In these years, Berkeley, University and town, achieved the creation of a unique culture, largely imported but adapted to the needs and wishes of California society.

The University by Wheeler's day had already abandoned all but a few vestiges of the traditional American college, which for 250 years had been based on religious piety; rote learning of the classics; a prescribed curriculum originally dividing all learning into moral, mental, and natural philosophy; and an overall commitment to building character. This model, mainly of New England origin, had been followed with surprising fidelity by the old College of California, which had maintained a precarious existence from 1855 to 1868. Like many of its predecessors all across the country, the College had been dominated by Yale men and heavily influenced by the Congregational-New School Presbyterian churches, the traditional sponsors of evangelical education and reform.[10] By mid-century, however, the old college pattern was dying fast even in its eastern homeland, and it had never been really compatible with the social, cultural, and religious climate of California. Despite some New England influence, the state had no tradition of dominant, established neo-Calvinist churches and lacked the hereditary gentry that had supported the old order in New England. Conservative religionists, usually Congregational or Presbyterian, looked back wistfully to the old College of California, and some of them regularly denounced the University as godless or Unitarian. By Wheeler's day, if not earlier, this kind of attack could be handled, though never dismissed. President Wheeler's own attitude toward religious pressures is revealingly stated in a letter from him to Henry Morse Stephens, head of the history department. Wheeler is commenting on an article by Preserved Smith, a liberal historian of ideas and religion, on "The Methods of Reformation Interpreters of the Bible." Wheeler admires the article and its author but concludes:

> I am afraid it would never do to make him a professor in the University outright because of the very ticklish character of his subject. In spite of the utterly scientific method of his procedure, one denomination or another would surely take exception, if not to the facts, at least to his balance. . . . We are going on very comfortably now and perhaps it is better not to kick a slumbering dog.[11]

Except for a surviving strong emphasis on classics, the University of California of Wheeler's day had long rejected the old college pattern. Instead, it was now a combination of three of the models distinguished by Veysey, the models that were sometimes competing, sometimes combining in the emergence of the American university. These were, first, the democratic and utilitarian people's university; second, the stronghold of polite traditional culture, and third, the center of high-powered and specialized research. Let us look briefly at each of these before we go on to our main topic, the way in which all three conflicting ideals were more or less harmoniously combined in Wheeler's Berkeley.

First, despite the fact that it had had to fight off extreme attacks from populist and practicalist forces, the University always was and had to be to some extent both democratic and utilitarian. From the start, it had rejected tuition and its spokesmen, including Wheeler, prided themselves on the large number of poor and working students. Of course, there were also many students who were not poor and some from the region's rich and prestigious families.[12]

Almost at the start, in 1870, the regents had resolved "that young ladies be admitted into the university on equal terms with young men," and a similar provision had been placed in the state constitution by the legislature in the basic act concerning University government in 1879.[13] Through the rest of the century the percentage of women lagged, slowly gaining in the 1890s. By 1900, however, women constituted 46 percent of the student body. At the end of his career, President Wheeler boasted that women "have had every advantage that the University has to offer from the beginning of the University's life."[14] Equality in admissions and in formal academic opportunities was impressive, in a period when both Michigan and Stanford had quotas and Chicago separate classes, to say nothing of the major eastern all-male universities. Of course, this sort of formal equality did not protect women students at California from harassment, insult, and unspoken restriction.[15] Genuinely believing in what they saw as equal education for women, Wheeler and his chief lieutenants were men of their time in their attitudes toward the purposes of female education. Wheeler himself thought that women should be trained primarily to carry out their special vocation as wives, mothers, and household managers. In 1914 he was glad to support the organization of a home economics department, which was strongly supported by the few women faculty members, including Jessica Peixotto, the first woman professor, and Lucy Ward Stebbins, the second Dean of Women.[16] Wheeler took it for granted that most student activities were for males, and student government, with Wheeler's enthusiastic approval, was dominated by senior men.

Henry Morse Stephens of history, Wheeler's favorite department head, had a similar attitude. Asserting the equal dignity of all kinds of student preparations and purposes, Stephens in 1919 clearly differentiated between the goals of males and females:

> I believe it to be of immense value that young men who are going to be architects or engineers or agriculturists should live and study with young men who are interested in Philosophy and History and Literature. I believe it to be of immense value that young women who are training to be good wives in the Home Economics Department should live with girls who are going to be teachers or nurses or physicians.[17]

As some realms of study were closed to women in practice, others were perceived as especially appropriate for them. Charles Mills Gayley, the immensely popular teacher of literature, was attacked by feminists in the *Daily Californian* for giving separate sections of his Great Books courses for men and women. His defense was that he especially wanted to attract engineers, who were likely to believe literature unmanly and sometimes had to come to class in dirty clothes.[18]

Most women who did not come to the University looking forward to marriage and children intended to be teachers. The President's Report for 1915-16, Wheeler's last before the changes brought by war, finds 388 women in the College of Letters and Science, one in the College of Commerce, two in Agriculture, and none in Mechanics, Civil Engineering, or Chemistry. In graduate study there was a little more diversity. There were 422 women in Letters and Science, 39 in agriculture, 28 in Chemistry, 26 in Medicine, 16 in Jurisprudence, and a tiny scattering in other fields.[19]

Whatever the tacit qualifications, the University in its own eyes was devoted to equal education for all classes and both sexes. Similarly, nobody disputed its commitment to some kinds of public service, especially service to the state's agriculture. The Morrill Act of 1862 in words that had insured endless debates over their interpretation, stated that the purpose of its grant of lands was to endow in each state an institution "where the leading object shall be, without excluding other scientific and classical studies, and including military tactics, to teach such branches of learning as are related to agriculture and the mechanic arts." Even beyond the college of agriculture and the professional schools, the importance of public service was emphasized by many departments, including economics and political science, both formed (by fission from history) in the Wheeler period.[20]

The opposite—in some of its spokesmen the militant opposite— to the democratic-utilitarian program was the tradition of polite culture, surprisingly strong from the start and perhaps reaching its height in the Wheeler period. Polite, or liberal, or traditional culture was then as always hard to define. For some it was an indefinable but recognizable essence, without which society was likely to become coarse or dehumanized. For some it was one or another form of moral idealism, necessary to combat American materialism. For most defenders of traditional culture, what was at stake was continuity with the past, and few doubted that this meant the European past. For many, the model of culture was Harvard, to which some California departments had a colonial relation in this period. Others would not settle for any model closer than Oxford or Cambridge. These loyalties, often expressed, increased the hostility of egalitarian opponents of polite culture. For many

10

Californians, the British universities and still more, Harvard, were favorite symbols of effete eastern snobbery.

For many of its defenders, traditional culture was centered, as it always had been, in knowledge of the Greek and Latin classics.[21] From the days of the College of California on, the classics had hung on to their position of special privilege. A knowledge of Greek and Latin was required for an A.B. at Berkeley until 1915, though by then it had become possible to escape the classical language requirement by opting for a Bachelorship of Letters or of Social Science. When, over a number of dead bodies, this distinction was ended and the language requirement dropped in 1915, one distinguished classicist lamented the change. Up to now, he said, he had always been able to tell the A.B. candidates from the others, because they looked more intelligent and refined.[22] Through the Wheeler period, classics at Berkeley were fed by the high schools. All of these offered and supported Latin, many Greek as well. The importance of the classics at Berkeley is further suggested by the power of classicists in the administration. Wheeler's predecessor, President Martin Kellogg, had started as a professor of Latin. Wheeler during most of his early career taught mainly Greek. Leon J. Richardson, of the Latin Department, was from 1901 head of the University committee that accredited schools and naturally insisted on the importance of his own subject.[23] Monroe Deutsch, appointed by Wheeler as a Latin professor, became vice-president in 1930. Deutsch was devoted to Wheeler's memory and tried to maintain intact the Wheeler tradition.

In a letter of 1900 Wheeler eloquently states his devotion to Greek language and culture. He rejoices that Greek language study is growing both in the high schools and the University.

While I cannot insist that a knowledge of Greek is an absolute essential for a liberal education, I still think that for the young man who has mental clearness and taste for the better things, it is the safer course to include Greek among his studies. For the purposes of the higher taste— culture, it may even be reasonably said that of the two classical languages, the one that is to be preserved if but one can be taught is Greek.[24]

The classics were taught well in this period, surely far better than in the rote-learning days of the College of California. Partly through Wheeler's urging, Mrs. Jane K. Sather established a classical lecture series that was to become one of the most prestigious in the world. The first eight incumbents, like all faculty, were appointed by President Wheeler.[25]

The most interesting representative of classical culture in Wheeler's Berkeley was Arthur William Ryder, brought to Berkeley in 1906 to teach Sanskrit[26] (Figure 2). Ryder thought that instruction at the University should consist primarily of Latin, Greek, and mathematics. A few rewards like Sanskrit should be available to those who were really well grounded in these basic fields. A loner with a caustic wit, Ryder was also a really gifted poet, epigrammatist, and translator. He was outspoken in his contempt for the dry scholarship of articles with too many footnotes— Sanskrit should be studied not for philological reasons but for the great literature it opened. His dramatic verse translations of Sanskrit classics were performed not only in the Greek Theater but in New York. Throughout the Wheeler period and for 20 years after, he taught a few students to whom he willingly offered all he had. One of his devoted auditors in his last years was Robert Oppenheimer, who learned to read the language and was to greet the dawn of the nuclear age with an apocalyptic Sanskrit quotation. Appropriately, Ryder died in 1938 while teaching an advanced class with one student.

Of course not all classicists, and certainly not all spokesmen of polite culture at Berkeley, were Ryders. Some, like the Custodians of Culture elsewhere in the country, could be pom-

Arthur William Ryder

pous, timid, and rigid. This fact does not, of course, immediately invalidate all their arguments. And even if one rejects all of these, I think that one has to see a certain narrow nobility in the defense of deeply treasured values against very real attack. Some contemporaries found the Berkeley version of polite culture more relaxed, less formal, less stuffy than its eastern original.

Veysey's third model, the all-out quest for research achievement, was rapidly gaining ground all over the country in this period of increasing wealth and specialization. Believers in research appealed to the German rather than the British example, and some defenders of literary culture condemned them for exactly this reason. Of course high-level research, especially in fields such as astronomy, which seemed to have no immediate practical consequences, was attacked and caricatured by extreme believers in the democratic-utilitarian tradition.

The first powerful Berkeley spokesman of the new research tradition was Daniel Coit Gilman, whose inaugural in 1872 was an eloquent plea for the University as "a group of agencies organized to advance the arts and sciences of every sort, and to train young men as scholars for all the intellectual callings of life."[27] This was too elitist a vision for much of the California public, and Gilman was charged with godlessness, downgrading the mechanical arts, and currying favor with the rich. Partly because of this sort of turmoil, Gilman in 1874 accepted an offer to become the first president of the Johns Hopkins University. Gilman probably would have accepted this offer even if his tenure at Berkeley had been calmer. Hopkins promised to become the vanguard of the new German research tradition in America. California, at this time, had made only a start in this direction.

Twenty-five years later, Wheeler became president. Very proud of his own Heidelberg degree, he could hardly fail to respond to the growing demand that American universities follow the German lead. Moreover, he was deeply determined to put the University of California abreast of its eastern contemporaries, and research was fast becoming the chief currency of competition. Gradually, as he got his political base firmly established, he turned more and more in this direction. Looking back, a memoir by a history department member sums it up:

> The University during those days was in the process of changing from a college into a university, from teaching to research. This change was the task of Wheeler, and in it he could be somewhat ruthless.[28]

Major progress in research cost money, and Wheeler was very fortunate in the benefactors he found and cultivated. Most of these came from the San Francisco rich. In the early decades of the University this group was too busy with the struggle for power to be much interested in supporting local culture. By Wheeler's day, however, some of them, especially women of wealth and leisure, had arrived at a stage of stability and confidence that enabled them to interest themselves in philanthropy. Obviously, this stage had been reached far earlier in Boston, New York, and Chicago. Some of the San Francisco patrons of the University interested themselves, with devotion and intelligence, in particular fields, not necessarily fields with obvious utilitarian payoff. One thinks immediately of Jane K. Sather in classics and history and Phoebe Apperson Hearst in many fields, most notably anthropology, a department she created, developed, and for its first seven years financed out of her own pocket. There were many other important donors.

The research emphasis led in two directions. First, professors with their own funds and direct links to wealthy patrons sometimes became more independent from administrative control than Wheeler had intended. Second, a research criterion for appointment or promotion pointed in the direction of judgment by experts, and in the long run toward the doctrine of the independence and presumed equality of all fields. Secretly, no doubt, many professors, both scientists and humanists, really thought that their own fields were central and superior, but it became a tactical necessity not to say so. These developments, however, were only getting under way in the Wheeler years; as a modern research university, California was in the process of emerging.

I come finally to my main question: How were these three models successfully combined at California in the Wheeler period? A full answer to this question would demand a study of the social and economic history of the state. Like the rest of the country, California was about to emerge from the angry turmoil of the nineties into the comparative social peace of the Progressive Era. The battle against the Southern Pacific, on which California politics centered, was long and hard, but the crucial encounters were won by middle-class reformers within the Republican Party.[29] The social and financial leadership of the state was concentrated in the San Francisco region. Wheeler's own political views were on the conservative edge of Progressivism, a fact that helped him develop cordial and fruitful relations with the more liberal-minded of the San Francisco rich. Cordial and fruitful, but not subservient: his idea of his own dignity and that of his position made that impossible. When, at Berkeley's rival institution, Mrs. Leland Stanford forced the president to dismiss Edward Albion Ross, a controversial sociologist and immigration theorist, Wheeler in a private letter expressed his strong disapproval. No doubt, he conceded, Ross had been partisan and unscientific. On the other hand, there was even less doubt that he had been ousted because of Mrs. Stanford's opinion of his teachings. "This is most unfortunate. It is indeed thoroughly bad. We must resist the tendency of wealth to tell the University what it shall teach."[30] The proper person to determine this was, of course, the president.

Wheeler himself was part of the reason for the success of Berkeley in reconciling three major traditions. He had indeed some claim to embody all three. He had come to Berkeley from Cornell, then associated with a practical bent and a tradition in agricultural research, and he never forgot the University's long-run dependence on public opinion. He had a German degree in comparative philology. At Cornell he had taught Sanskrit as well as Greek.[31] (Perhaps this partly explains his support of Ryder, surely not his favorite kind of professor.)

Wheeler comes off badly in Veysey's *Emergence*, as he would in any account stressing the history of ideas.[32] As with many of his contemporaries among men of action and builders of institutions, his actions are much more interesting than his words. Read in cold blood, most of Wheeler's presidential speeches and other writings are banal and conventional in the extreme and not without a strong note of anti-intellectualism. He repeatedly insists that he prefers the gregarious, sociable, all-round man, either as student or professor, to the radical, the idealist, or the cloistered scholar. (It should be noted that he protected some individuals who belonged in the latter categories.) The single general idea he most often expresses is a belief in an organic society, in his period a view that went against the traditional individualist rhetoric dominant in America but yet had its very influential sponsors like Herbert Croly. "We are first and foremost social beings; we are animals of the pack. . . . We have got to share our lives with others in order to have them normal."[33]

In his first Berkeley speech he stated a similar view in more emotional terms: "We are a family. You cannot make a university out of minds and brains. In a university, as elsewhere in life, heart is more than head, love is more than reason."[34] In this one sentiment, though nowhere else, the Berkeley rebels of the 1960s might have agreed with him.

17

It is not surprising that his political ideal was summed up by Theodore Roosevelt, who shared many of his tastes and viewpoints. Probably the high point of Wheeler's presidency came in 1903 when Roosevelt accepted his invitation to give the Berkeley commencement speech (Figure 3). The president of the University writes to the president of the United States with an informality proper between friendly potentates:

> If you can, arrange to be with us on the night before Commencement. We will get up early in the morning and have a gallop over the magnificent hills which give us our background and overlook the Bay and Gate.[35]

Throughout the rest of Roosevelt's presidency, Wheeler wrote him regularly, expressing his opinions on appointments and policies.

In his own sphere, Wheeler was a master politician. Indeed, his political realism and skill were his essential and outstanding equipment for his difficult job. Knowing the fate of some of his predecessors and the University's reputation as a president-eater, he demanded, before he would accept the presidency, certain essential guarantees from the regents:

(1) That the President should be in *fact*, as in theory, the sole organ of communication between Faculty and Regents;

(2) That the President should have sole initiative in appointments and removals of professors and other teachers and in matters affecting salary;

(3) That the Board, however divided in opinion during discussion, should in all things the President is called upon to do regarding the Faculty, support him as a unit;

(4) That the President should be charged with the direction, subject to the Board, of all officers and employees of the University.[36]

Photo Courtesy
Oakland Tribune

Two Presidents

As he got the regents' confidence, decisions in these all-important matters became in fact mainly his own. He was an indefatigable and, for most audiences, an effective public speaker and proved able to call upon the pride of the people of California in their university—a pride that was always strong, if often ambivalent. Soon he became a major public figure in the state.

Very early, Wheeler was able to gain the support of another crucial element—the students. From his first speech in Berkeley he expressed a warm affection for the undergraduates and a concern for their interests. Many anecdotes of alumni suggest that the president, usually a formal and even somewhat pompous figure, found himself able to unbend and to show his feelings most easily with students. Wheeler's period and the next saw the heyday of the alma mater spirit—the devotion of students and alumni to the site, the teams, the songs, and the traditions (sometimes created to order) of the institution. College spirit is obviously from an administration point of view a great good thing, but in American academic history it has frequently gotten out of hand. From the 1790s to the 1950s far more destruction and mayhem were caused by nonpolitical rows and riots, explicable only by an excess of youthful mass emotion, than by any with expressed political purposes.

Wheeler was a past master at supporting, channeling, and containing college spirit. Riding around the campus on his horse in true Rooseveltian style, he was able to greet many undergraduates by their first names. They were always welcome to come to his office hours. He never missed a game or rally. He promoted student government in particular, leaving senior men large powers to deal with disciplinary matters. The students—perhaps especially male students— enthusiastically approved.

With the regents, the benefactors, the public, and the students behind him, Wheeler was free to mold a faculty as he

20

chose. His methods were those of a benevolent despot. Everybody on the faculty agreed about the despotism. Opinions about the benevolence varied a bit. He determined most curricular matters and policed the behavior of junior faculty, insisting that appointments must be kept and leaves given only for very serious reasons. According to one perfectly plausible legend, he once reproved a faculty member for appearing on the campus without a hat.[37] Despite all this, it is clear that many faculty members liked and admired the president.

Once Wheeler found a department head with whom he was entirely comfortable, he encouraged consultation and suggestions. He often gave trusted subordinates cordial support in matters of junior appointments, salaries, and equipment. In such matters, however, all power of decision remained firmly in the president's hands. Writing to G. H. Howison of philosophy, one of his most trusted and admired department chiefs, Wheeler says in 1906 of one young visitor to the philosophy department:

> I visited Dr. X's lecture, and I, myself thought it represented in tone and mode of presentation a close imitation of a Sunday School concert address. . . . I should think . . . therefore, there could be no possible consideration of Dr. X as a candidate for the vacant position.[38]

Two years later, he reports that he has failed on his annual eastern trip to make contact with a junior candidate Howison has suggested: "I should very much dislike to recommend for appointment here a man whom I had never seen."[39]

What was the basis of Wheeler's faculty selection? First, a professor must be a gentleman.[40] This is a term harder to define in American than in European social history. Family origins were not really central. Many professors were sons of ministers. It is not hard to find a few whose fathers were small merchants who had never been to college. What was essential was correct speech and manners, conversational ability, and some knowledge of literature— preferably starting with the classics, certainly including the principal English authors. Religion was no longer crucial as long as one did not hold either fervently evangelical or militantly atheistic views.[41] Faculty religion in general ranged from liberal Protestantism to quasi-theistic idealism. From 1902 to 1910, the Berkeley faculty even included Jacques Loeb, a distinguished biologist who was the country's most famous and outspoken protagonist of rigorous naturalistic mechanism. A Berkeley memoir reports, however, that neither Loeb's views nor his personality made him popular and that this had some relation to his departure for the Rockefeller Institute of Medical Research.[42]

In a few cases, ladies were acceptable instead of gentlemen. From the time Phoebe Apperson Hearst became a regent in 1897, she started promoting the idea of appointing women faculty. After some halfway measures (such as a female physician and lecturer in hygiene paid for by Mrs. Hearst), Wheeler broached a bolder step. In 1904 he wrote Henry Morse Stephens, the head of history, enclosing, "a sort of syllabus of some lectures that Miss Jessica Peixotto, Ph.D., has been recently giving in the city. She is a brilliant woman, and ought in some way to be utilized by the University."[43] Peixotto was of Portuguese Jewish descent. She was the daughter of a rich and philanthropic San Francisco businessman and had received the second Ph.D. granted to a woman by Berkeley. Apparently there was no appropriate spot in history, and Wheeler, who never cared a lot about academic boundaries, appointed her a lecturer in sociology in 1904. She soon moved to economics, where she had a long, productive, and distin-guished career.[44]

The second woman to be appointed was Lucy Sprague, a close personal friend of the Wheelers[45] (Figure 4). A Radcliffe graduate from an upper-class Chicago family, Sprague had good

22

Dean Lucy Sprague

looks, at once elegant and somewhat ethereal social charm, keen literary interests, and a serious though not radical interest in social reform. As her biographer says, "She came from the social and intellectual circle with which Wheeler was most comfortable."[46]

Wheeler wanted to appoint his young protegée dean of women. Sprague did not have much formal graduate training, a fact about which she always felt self-conscious. She insisted that before becoming dean she should have faculty experience, so Wheeler gave her an appointment first in English, then in economics.

When she finally became dean of women in 1906, Lucy Sprague proved vigorous and effective. Her principal purpose was to break with the dominant assumption that women came to college either to marry or to become teachers. Some found her, in fact, less interested in prospective teachers than in other students. Trying to give them some of her own diverse tastes and interests, she invited students to her house on Ridge Road for literary readings and also took them to San Francisco to visit orphanages, poorhouses, and the docks. In the manner of some feminists and reformers of her time, she was strongly in favor of franker discussion of sexual issues and problems such as venereal disease. Because women were excluded from most undergraduate activities, she organized a dance drama, the Partheneia, which was written, directed, and acted by women.[47] Sprague played a prominent role in Berkeley social life, and before long she found a kindred spirit in Wesley Mitchell, an important institutional economist. Gradually they fell in love and, on a faculty Sierra trip, decided to get married. Once married, in 1912 they decided they wanted to live in New York, the center of both social reform and literary experiment. Sprague was devoted to Wheeler and felt that he was always supportive of her mildly feminist purposes.

If Wheeler, within limits, was friendly to women faculty, some male professors were not. Both Peixotto and Sprague report that they were coolly received in many faculty quarters. Neither ever mustered the courage to attend a faculty meeting. While some social circles warmly welcomed them, they like all women were excluded, significantly, from the Kosmos Club, the leading faculty society. According to one memoirist, this was "on account of the smoking problem."[48] Men obviously had to smoke; ladies could not enjoy a smoky atmosphere.

In 1917, Wheeler's last year, I find only five women faculty members outside of home economics and hygiene.[49] The total number of faculty members was 329.

In appointing ethnic minorities Wheeler was a little ahead of his times.[50] At Berkeley Jews were not barred, and some of them, like Jessica Peixotto and Monroe Deutsch, achieved success and recognition. Then, as later, there was a good deal less anti-Semitism at Berkeley than in leading eastern universities. California specialized rather in barring Asians. I can find only one Asian of faculty rank, an instructor in Japanese, in the list of faculty in the 1917-18 catalogue. I find only three southern Europeans, two Italians, and one Spaniard, all serving in language departments at low ranks. The important point here is that the overwhelming majority of the faculty, in Berkeley as elsewhere throughout the country, were white males of Northern European Protestant origin. And all exceptions, female or ethnic outsider, had to satisfy the all-important requirement of gentility.[51]

After gentility, the next basic requirement was vigorous and successful undergraduate teaching. Wheeler certainly did not want either students or their parents dissatisfied. But after this, and increasingly important, was scholarly achievement. As he became more and more secure, Wheeler became capable of waiving the first two requirements, at least partially, in cases of real research distinction. And one has to concede that Wheeler had an instinct for distinction.

This is the only possible explanation for the undoubted fact that Wheeler's system of faculty recruiting, for all its arbitrariness, worked remarkably well. Were there, then, giants in those days? Certainly, but to avoid too much nostalgia, we should remember one of Ryder's most caustic witticisms. Seeing at the faculty club Henry Morse Stephens surrounded by several members of the history department, Ryder said, "There goes a fake giant surrounded by real pygmies."[52] Whether or not this remark is too hard on Stephens, and I think it is, there were among the Berkeley faculty in those days all kinds of giants, real and fake. There were also some faculty members who were both, people who had flamboyant personalities that they exploited to the full and who also had real ability of one kind or another. And of course, there were many who did not pretend to be giants at all.

A few of Wheeler's appointments with considerable claim to one kind or another of gigantism might include Stephens, Herbert E. Bolton, and F. J. Teggart in history, Bernard Moses in political science, Charles Kofoid in zoology, Griffith Evans in mathematics, Herbert Evans in biology, and A. L. Kroeber in anthropology. An appointment that was very important in Berkeley history was that of John Galen Howard in 1903 as the first head of the School of Architecture and the University's supervising architect during its greatest architectural flowering.[53]

Another Wheeler appointment that deserves special mention is that of Gilbert Lewis, who in 1911 was brought to Berkeley from M.I.T. to build up graduate study in chemistry (Figure 5). Lewis, a handsome, brilliant, sometimes arrogant Harvard man, was a typical Wheeler selection.[54] Perhaps because Wheeler did not know enough about Lewis's field to interfere a lot, Lewis expected and got more autonomy than most of Wheeler's lieutenants. As a condition of accepting

Gilbert N. Lewis

Wheeler's invitation, he demanded and got four new faculty appointments, eight staff assistants, and the promise of a building. Between 1915 and 1937 all Berkeley chemistry appointments were Berkeley Ph.D.s. Apparently this inbreeding did not work badly: Berkeley chemistry was to produce seven Nobel laureates, five of them Berkeley Ph.D.s. (Lewis himself, to his great chagrin, was never selected for a Nobel award). Disliking lab minutiae and never intensely interested in administration, Lewis restricted his own teaching to presiding over a famous weekly research conference for faculty and graduate students. Unprepared or foolish comments could produce searing rejoinders, but students who had done their work well were allowed to challenge their formidable chairman. Far-ranging and imaginative, Lewis described his field as nonspecialized, mainly mathematical physics. His interests ranged through chemistry, physics, and even biology. This breadth as well as his sheer talent put Lewis in a position to make the greatest single contribution to Berkeley's coming scientific greatness.

Writing to George Noyes of Slavic literature near the end of his own career, Wheeler recalls his purpose in starting the Slavic department (one of the first in the country) with the appointment of Noyes in 1901. The president had wanted the University, he said, to provide instruction in the language, thought, and history of all the great centers of learning in the world. These indispensable cultures included the Chinese, Japanese, Indic, Arabic, Russian and other Slavic, Greek, Latin, Spanish, French, and German.[55] This was a far more catholic and less Europe-centered list than that of many university statesmen of Wheeler's day. Wheeler's star appointments were sometimes made at the beginning of a candidate's career, and sometimes a leading professor was persuaded to leave another university. The list included really creative scientists, highly talented humanists, and even reclusive scholars. But his own

real favorites were the all-round men, whether he had appointed them or found them in Berkeley when he came. Some of
these were people of expressive, even flamboyant personality, a
type then more acceptable among professors than now. Some
helped enormously to bring together utility, culture, and research. I will briefly discuss just four of these especially
valuable and versatile individuals. In extremely different ways,
all were big figures in the community and state as well as in the
University.

The two most *visible* members of Wheeler's faculty were
Henry Morse Stephens of history and Charles Mills Gayley of
English. Stephens was a Scot from an Indian army family and
had an excellent English education culminating in a First in
Modern History at Balliol College, Oxford[56] (Figure 6). He was
a prolific writer, both as a newspaper critic of literature and the
arts and as a historian. During his early career he wrote books
on the history of France, Portugal, Europe in general, and
India. He was called to Cornell in 1894. In 1902 his friend
Wheeler persuaded him to come to Berkeley as Sather Professor
of History, Director of Extension, and head of the history
department.

Stephens was Wheeler's closest faculty friend. In their long
correspondence he was addressed as "Dear Professor Stephens"
in official letters, "My Dear Stephens" in more personal notes.
However, in 1917, when Stephens was ill in the East, Wheeler
started a letter as "My dearly beloved Stephens" and signs
himself "ever yours." Still more startling, on January 8, 1917,
Wheeler signed a get-well telegram "Benjamin," the only use of
his first name I have seen except in letters to elderly relatives.[57]
Yet Stephens' requests for appointments or supplies were by no
means always granted—no more so than those of other leading
heads of departments.

Henry Morse Stephens

Within the history department Stephens ran a very tight ship and was by no means universally popular.[58] In his various administrative positions Stephens stood for authority, equity, and uniform rules, especially for junior faculty. He was an enemy of inconsistencies in such matters as grading, hours of work, and employment of readers.

With considerable assiduousness, Stephens directly courted the support of rich patrons of culture, sometimes eluding, in a good cause, Wheeler's prohibition against direct contact between faculty and regents. Among many successes in getting philanthropic support, he played the principal role in securing for the University Hubert Howe Bancroft's vast library of Californian and western history. Stephens' philanthropic friends also provided funds for the library's upkeep. Though his own early interests had not pointed particularly toward Hispanic history, he was the person most responsible for the University's major turn in that direction. He persuaded Wheeler to call Herbert Eugene Bolton from Stanford in 1910 and went on to add three more appointments in California and Hispanic history. He secured fellowships for graduate students to work in Spanish archives and corresponded, sometimes in Spanish, with Spanish and Latin-American scholars. In 1915, in connection with the San Francisco Panama-Pacific Exposition, Stephens successfully promoted a Hispanic History Congress, securing Theodore Roosevelt as one of the speakers.

In terms of the three ideologies competing in Berkeley and other universities, one might initially put Stephens on the side of the research tradition. He was elected president of the American Historical Association in 1915 and had a reputation for insisting on meticulous use of sources. However, in dealing with appointments, he often came down strongly on the side of culture. Recommending a graduate student to the president of Reed College, he makes light of the candidate's lack of a doctoral degree: "As an old Oxford man myself I have always

laid much more stress upon a man's cultivation and teaching
ability than upon the actual obtaining of a' Ph.D. degree."[59]

Yet culture too could be waived. In 1912, recommending
a successor to his own headship of extension, he recommended
to Wheeler a man from the Wisconsin extension, which
represented the epitome of public service as against traditional
culture:

> He seems to me to be a typical middle western
> hustler; he is not afraid of getting out among the
> farmers and is acquainted with extension work in
> agriculture; he could go to all sorts of places and
> organize all sorts of centers, where I could not and did
> not. He does not appeal to me personally as either a
> fine-grained gentleman or as a scholar; he has only his
> B.A. degree from Wisconsin; he is the country high
> school type; but he understands the Wisconsin idea
> and could develop our department along Wisconsin
> lines.[60]

In 1919, at the time of Wheeler's retirement, Stephens
wrote to a friend on the Board of Regents that in a modern,
democratic university, "There is nothing to be gained by
clinging to the old tradition of Latin, Greek, and Mathematics."[61]

Much of Stephens' immense energy in his Berkeley period
went to his promotion of student government and to his
lectures, eloquently delivered and thoroughly standard in
content. An easy and versatile public lecturer, Stephens was
much in demand in the state and nation. To a woman in
Milwaukee who was trying to arrange an appearance for him he
suggested that he might lecture on "the Social Interpretation of
History," on St. Francis, or on Robespierre.[62] He found time
also to read aloud from the works of Kipling, to whom he was
passionately devoted, to the Berkeley Lions' Club.[63]

Charles Mills Gayley was generally thought in Berkeley to be somehow British (Figure 7). Actually he was born in Shanghai of American missionary parents.[64] He attended an English school in Ireland and then the University of Michigan, where he became an instructor in 1880. His political loyalties were not English but Ascendancy Irish, and in his early life he supported both Irish independence and the Gaelic League. He was, however, fervently devoted to English literary culture. When war came in 1914, Gayley, like many American lovers of English literature, became violently pro-British and hostile to the lukewarm. His own poetry was thoroughly English in manner, occasionally political in a Kiplingesque manner, sometimes quasi-mystical in the style of the contemporary Georgians.[65]

Gayley was a pure specimen of the believer in classical and traditional culture. Before coming to Berkeley from Michigan in 1889, he had taught Latin and translated from Greek. His most popular work, *Classic Myths in English Literature*, was a rewriting of Bulfinch's *Age of Fable* for use in the schools. In his essays, like other Custodians of Culture then and later, he lamented the collapse of American civilization that was inevitably being brought about by the loosening of classical training.[66] He heartily disliked the German scholarly tradition and blamed its growing strength in America on Charles William Eliot of Harvard.[67]

Gayley, who constantly proclaimed his allegiance to the ideals of classical culture and had little use for the other two major university traditions, does not fit the pattern of eclectic reconciliation especially favored by Wheeler. Yet he was not like other custodians of culture either. There was no trace in him of the reclusive or fastidious scholar on the model of Arthur Ryder. His works were anything but esoteric or austerely classical. His literary role was that of appreciator and transmitter, and he was in demand as a public lecturer. One

Charles Mills Gayley

of his favorite lectures dealt with "Shakespeare and the Found-
ers of Liberty in America."

None of the tendency to deplore or disapprove that one can
find in his works comes across in contemporary accounts of
Gayley's personality. Indeed, he seems to have been universally
liked in his department, in faculty society, and among the
students. In his department he befriended junior faculty
members and left a tradition of the involvement of senior
professors in undergraduate teaching. His friends considered
him a brilliant conversationalist and raconteur.

Above all, Gayley was a charismatic undergraduate teacher.
His Great Books course, covering everything from the Indian
epics and Plato to Sienkiewicz, was so popular that he had to
give it in the Greek Theater. He carefully filed student
comments from the *Daily Californian*. These were many and
almost always favorable, though it was occasionally suggested
that his courses were undemanding. Gayley was an eager
supporter of student debating and, perhaps more surprisingly,
of football. He was the author of one of California's most
popular football songs and had earlier written one of Michigan's. On a return visit to Michigan in 1925 he was overjoyed
to find that his song, composed in the mid-1880s, was still
being sung. His statement about this is revealing and poignant:

A song written in the days of one's youth, if it by
good luck expresses the devotion and enthusiasm of
succeeding generations of young men and women, is a
thousand times more worthwhile than many books of
learning produced with much labor in after years by
anyone who, like myself, has never been able to go
ahead with his early poetic ambitions because he has
had to make a stab at proving himself a scholar.[68]

Two other professors, neither of them anything like
Stephens or Gayley, were more important than either as
reconcilers and unifiers. Both were at Berkeley before Wheeler

came, but he relied heavily on both. One of these was George Holmes Howison of philosophy[69] (Figure 8). Howison came from Ohio and spent part of his earlier career teaching in St. Louis, the American headquarters of Hegelian idealism. He was however deeply under the spell of Harvard and especially of William James. In the 1870s and early 1880s, he found teaching and lecturing positions in the Boston area, hoping desperately for a Harvard appointment. In 1883 he wasbeaten out at Harvard by Josiah Royce, who had long been bitterly unhappy in the Berkeley English department and was overjoyed to accept a Harvard instructorship in philosophy.

In 1884 President Reid of California offered Howison the newly endowed Mills Professorship of Philosophy and the department chairmanship, with the task of building a first-rate department from scratch. Howison's Harvard friends, William James and George Palmer, urged him to accept, though both expressed a low opinion of the university at Berkeley. More or less graciously, Howison embarked on a lifetime of exile. Palmer and James both kept in confidential and intimate touch with Howison, and philosophy at Berkeley gradually became a favored colony of Harvard in the Golden Age of Harvard philosophy. Howison sent his best students to Harvard for graduate work, and Harvard sent instructors to California for testing by experience.

As a philosopher, Howison was more than respectable. His doctrine of personal or plural idealism has left few traces, but in its day it was well-regarded by James, Royce, and many others. As a graduate teacher, Howison was highly successful, training a number of distinguished philosophers such as A. O. Lovejoy of Hopkins. He built an impressive department, and in Wheeler's day had so much prestige that he usually presided at faculty meetings when Wheeler was in the East.

Some students and junior colleagues found Howison pompous and intimidating, and he was certainly as dictatorial

George Holmes Howison

in his sphere as Wheeler in his. The wife of an instructor describes him as a holy terror and regarded his dinner parties as ordeals. One instructor, she reports, had been dismissed from his job because he nervously pulled out a cigarette at the Howison's dinner table.[70] Yet Howison's papers contain ample, indeed overwhelming evidence of affection and esteem on the part of many students, both undergraduate and graduate. They also make clear his deep loyalty to them and his paternal concern for their careers.

In religious terms, Howison was exactly right for the Bay Area in his day. Trained as a minister, he had long left Christian orthodoxy behind, but remained theistic in a liberal and idealistic way. He was regularly denounced, as the University itself long had been, by conservative churchmen, but his files are full of letters from San Francisco businessmen and lawyers as well as students who felt that his teachings had saved their faith.

Howison's major contribution to the community was his Philosophic Forum, an organization whose mission was to further the serious but nontechnical study of current philosophic theories and problems by academics and laymen together. Most if not all of the country's most important philosophers, including Royce, James, Santayana, and Dewey, accepted invitations to speak. Perhaps the high point of the Forum came in 1896, shortly before Wheeler's arrival, when Royce, Royce's student Sidney Mezes, the venerable geologist Joseph Le Conte, and Howison himself discussed the question of the existence of God. Both God and freedom of inquiry came off reasonably well, the crowd was large, and the press reports highly favorable.[71]

Finally, the most valuable contributor to reconciliation and union of university ideologies in Berkeley was Eugene Woldemar Hilgard[72] (Figure 9). Hilgard was one of the leading agricultural scientists of his day. His father, a liberal jurist in

Eugene W. Hilgard

Bavaria, came to America for political reasons in 1836 when Eugene was three years old. Brought up in America, Hilgard returned to Germany for his training. After receiving his doctorate from Heidelberg, he spent two years in Spain, where he met his future wife and studied arid agriculture. Returning to the United States, he was successively employed by the Smithsonian Institution, the University of Mississippi, and the University of Michigan. In 1874 he was called to Berkeley by President Gilman as professor of agriculture and director of the agricultural experiment station. This was a front-line post, since the most devastating attacks on the University as useless and elitist were coming from farmers. Hilgard proved to be a fighter and an excellent political tactician. He was able to win the confidence of farmers by speaking to their organizations, without talking down, of the practical and immediate benefits afforded by agricultural science. But Hilgard's emphasis was not always or entirely utilitarian. His fundamental purpose was to insist that the study of agriculture in California must be serious science, not merely training in milking and plowing. A statement from a report of 1877 shows a combination of nine-teenth-century idealism and the classical tradition, drawn on by Jefferson among others, of rational agricultural improvement.

So long as they see in a farmer's life only the daily drudgery, without the cheerful background afforded to educated minds by the contact with nature, and the intellectual food so abundantly presented in the correct application of the principles governing the very complex profession of the truly rational farmers: so long will they continue in the vain attempt to find in our over-crowded cities a more satisfactory existence . . . it is clear that the remedy lies in the *elevation of the far-mer's pursuit to its true dignity* of a learned profession, second to none in the complexity and difficulty of the problems with which it deals, and superior to many in its fundamental importance, as well as in the rational enjoyment of life which it affords to those who under-stand the principles that underlie its practice. . . .[73]

Better than any other Berkeley professor, Hilgard brought together the three major traditions that were competing in Berkeley. With his German training, his six languages, his wide interests, and his social geniality, he was fully accepted by the local Custodians of Culture. Nobody could question either the utility of his work or the seriousness of his research. Howison and Hilgard make perfect symbols of the two sides of American culture proclaimed by Santayana, the idealistic and the practical, that divided between them the ethos of the Progressive Era.

That era, and Wheeler's Berkeley, which was so much a part of it, ended with the First World War. The war itself was the immediate cause of Wheeler's fall from power. In 1909-10 Wheeler had taken leave to serve as Theodore Roosevelt Professor at the University of Berlin. In presenting him to the Kaiser, the rector said that President Wheeler came from a monarchy in a democracy to visit a democracy in a monarchy.[74] The Kaiser was especially gracious, and Wheeler's long-standing admiration for German culture and institutions was reinforced.

From 1915 to 1917, as American participation in the war was hotly debated, Wheeler insisted in letters that the Kaiser was the greatest friend of peace, that the German army was a force for peace, and that he only wished England could understand this. He broke with his bellicose former idol, ex-President Roosevelt, to support Wilson as the peace candidate. In February 1917 he wrote his friend the Secretary of the Interior, Franklin K. Lane, that in his opinion nine out of 10 Americans were against war, with mainly "society people" on the other side. "Burlingame is for war. . . . Berkeley is for peace."[75] Up to the last moment he blamed Russia and England for the crisis.

When the United States finally went to war, Wheeler did all he could to support recruiting among the students and conversion of University resources to wartime functions. In the inflamed state of California wartime opinion, however, this was not enough. Inevitably, his enemies dug up his earlier pro-German statements, and in 1918 the regents created an Advisory Committee of Deans to "assist" Wheeler in carrying out his function. The members of this committee were Stephens, Gayley, and the Graduate Dean, William Carey Jones, all three impeccably and vociferously pro-Allied. Wheeler remained nominal president and in 1919, at 65, retired for reasons of diminishing health and energy.[76] He received full honors, and lived until 1927 the happy and active life of an elder statesman, commenting freely on University issues and never missing a football game.

Even without the war, however, Wheeler's system could not have lasted. The balance between intellectual distinction and democratic commitment, always the main problem for American high culture, could not be maintained in its exact prewar form either in Berkeley or in the nation, but had to be as it must be from time to time renegotiated in new terms. Both student and faculty numbers had tripled in Wheeler's time, and the University could no longer be run as a family under the president's all-seeing paternal eye. Regardless of size, Wheeler had built a faculty much too able and independent-minded to accept a childlike role. Henry Morse Stephens, among others, understood this. He said, "I am quite clear that no single human being can be President of the University of California in the sense in which President Wheeler was President when he first came to the University."[77]

The faculty had for some time showed signs of restiveness and with the popular paternal figure gone the time had come for change. The famous faculty revolt of 1919 led to the regents' New Standing Orders of 1920. These established the

powers of the Academic Senate and its committees in something like their present form and gave the faculty a major share
in decisions about appointments and promotions. Wheeler, in
a letter to President Hutchins of Michigan, commented in a
jocular rather than a bitter tone:

> Since I retired there has been a considerable
> overturning here in the direction of professorial Bolshe-
> vism. The faculty has had a joyous time in appointing
> its own committees and choosing its own Deans and
> exercising all sorts of outright and noble freedom.[78]

Many other changes of the postwar years altered the mores
of Wheeler's Berkeley. Social life was altered by Prohibition
and the automobile age and the look of the town by the fire of
1923. Yet many important customs, tastes, and practices from
that era remained essentially unchanged all the way through the
Bohemian twenties and troubled thirties and even through
World War II. Then came the successive and quite different
revolutions—at least they felt like revolutions—of the 1950s and
1960s.[79] After these, the University was much bigger, much
more distinguished, and much less contented.

Despite autocracy and its irritations, the University in the
Wheeler decades had been a happy ship. There is plenty of
evidence that most of the faculty[80] and most of the students
agreed with Wheeler's first and best-known statement as
president, "It is good to be here." Part of the reason for
general faculty contentment lay in something with which
Wheeler's policies had little direct connection. When eastern
professors were invited to move to Berkeley, they often made
their decision by balancing on one side remoteness from major
centers of culture and most equals in their fields against, on the
other side, the attractions of something they called "the California way of life."

The Berkeley faculty had indeed created a unique, autonomous, and remarkably pleasant way of life, provincial in a good

sense, a culture that deserves its historian. Visitors and newcomers usually found Berkeley life simpler, less formal, and less pretentious than the life of eastern university towns. There was a good reason for the simplicity: low salaries. As else-where in the country, full professors at Berkeley were paid far less than equally successful members of other professions, yet still enough, in this period of low prices, to sustain a decent and even modestly comfortable way of life.[81] Faculty members in the lower ranks had a hard struggle to make ends meet. In compensation for relative poverty, faculty positions brought some prestige and considerable leisure.

A vigorous club life was shared with lawyers and business-men from San Francisco or the East Bay, some of them quite as interested in literature or history or contemporary affairs as their faculty friends. Relative poverty does not seem to have embarrassed Berkeley professors; indeed, some tended to boast about their simple way of life. Many accomplished prodigies of hiking in Marin County and the Sierra. (Four peaks are said to have been named after members of the English depart-ment.)[82] For urban pleasures, San Francisco, a cosmopolitan and sophisticated city with good music and theater and excellent restaurants, was only a ferry-ride away.

Glancing briefly at this picture, present-day Berkeleyans cannot easily avoid all nostalgia. Therefore it is important to remember the other side of the balance: the various kinds of narrowness, the snobberies no matter how subtle, the distance from the centers of innovation and dissent—in sum, the negative side of provincialism. Above all, one should bear in mind the complacency that was part of the contentment. In Berkeley, as in Progressive middle-class America, the virtues of the culture were inseparable from its limitations, and neither could last far into the twentieth century.

NOTES

1. Henry F. May, *The End of American Innocence* (New York, 1959).

2. See Harold Kirker, *Old Forms on a New Land: California Architecture in Perspective* (Niwot, Colorado, 1991); Gunther Barth, *Instant Cities* (New York, 1975).

3. George Santayana, "The Genteel Tradition in American Philosophy," in his *Winds of Doctrine* (New York, 1913, paperback 1957), 188.

4. Edwin E. Slosson, *Great American Universities* (New York, 1910), 148-49.

5. Chicago, 1965.

6. Laurence Veysey, "Stability and Experiment in the American Undergraduate Curriculum," in *Content and Context: Essays on College Education*, ed. Carl Kaysen (New York, 1973), 1. Professor Veysey, in a comment on this passage, sticks to his guns: "If the changes at the end of the 19th century produced three rival ideals or 'interests,' namely, utility, research, and culture, the changes of the 1950s witnessed only a gaining ground of research at the expense of the other two. This I wouldn't see as being as fundamental a change as the creation of the troika itself. Also, much of the later change was a growth in numbers, and that in itself wouldn't seem as so basic as a change in fundamental structure." As for the changes in the 1960s, these, Veysey believes, must be seen "as an attempt to create a genuine revolution within the university, but as one that failed." Veysey to author, July 18, 1991.

7. Verne Stadtman, *The University of California, 1868-1968* (New York, 1970), 81-83.

8. This is pointed out by Monroe E. Deutsch in his introduction to Benjamin Ide Wheeler, *The Abundant Life* (Berkeley, 1926), 25-26.

9. Verne Stadtman, *Centennial Record of the University of California* (Berkeley, 1965), 216, 271-72.

10. This dominance and its decline at Berkeley and elsewhere is covered by George M. Marsden, "The Soul of the American University," in *The Secularization of the Academy*, ed. George M. Marsden and Bradley J. Longfield (New York, 1992).

11. Wheeler to Stephens, February 22, 1916. Stephens Papers.

12. According to Lynn Gordon, *Gender and Higher Education in the Progressive Era* (New Haven, 1990), 53, about half the students in this period came from families of professionals or businessmen, the other half from families of miners or farmers. A report of President Wheeler of 1905-06 breaks the students origins down more precisely and shows only a little over 20 percent coming from families of farmers or miners. Gordon, 206.

13. Stadtman, *University*, 83.

14. Wheeler to H. S. Middlemiss, October 12, 1920. Wheeler Papers. For statistics of enrollment, see *Centennial Record*, 212-25.

15. This sort of discrimination at Berkeley is usefully covered by Gordon, Chapter 2. My treatment of this topic has also been influenced by comments made by Professor Geraldine Clifford on an earlier version of this essay.

16. Gordon, *Gender*, 68; *Centennial Record*, 84-85.

17. Stephens to R. J. Taussig, April 14, 1919. Stephens Papers.

18. Clipping from *Daily Californian*, Gayley Papers.

19. *President's Report* for 1916-17, 470-71.

20. This continuing tradition at Berkeley is helpfully described by Mary E. Cookingham, "Social Economics and Reform: Berkeley, 1906-1961," *History of Political Economy*, XIX (1987), 47-65.

21. Information about classics at Berkeley comes mainly from Joseph Fontenrose, *Classics at Berkeley: The First Century, 1869-1970* (Berkeley, 1982), an excellent department history.

22. Professor Joseph Merrill quoted in Fontenrose, *Classics*, 19.

23. See Transcript of Leon Richardson's oral history, "Berkeley Culture, etc."

24. Wheeler to Ethel Beverton, November 13, 1900. Wheeler Papers.

25. Sterling Dow, *A History of the Sather Lectures* (Berkeley, 1965), 37.

26. Information about Ryder comes largely from Fontenrose, *Classics*; the excellent introduction by George Noyes to Arthur William Ryder, *Original Poems, together with Translations from the Sanskrit* (Berkeley, 1939); and from Ryder's successor, Professor Murray Emeneau.

27. Quoted by Stadtman, 64. Stadtman gives an excellent account of Gilman's brief presidency.

28. Jacob Neibert Bowman, "Reminiscences of the University of California, 1906-" (Bancroft Library), 31.

29. See George E. Mowry, *The California Progressives* (Berkeley, 1951).

30. Wheeler to Hammond Lamont, November 10, 1900. Wheeler Papers.

31. Information from Professor Murray Emeneau.

32. Wheeler's personality remains elusive, partly because he was a shy and reticent man, but also because his personal papers are mostly lost. When he retired from the presidency in 1919, he bought and moved to the house on Ridge Road owned and formerly occupied by Lucy Sprague Mitchell. In 1923 this house, and in it the Wheeler papers, were destroyed by the great Berkeley fire. The papers that Wheeler left behind on the campus, those now in the Bancroft Library, are not

without interest but are mainly official. Occasional letters from Wheeler in the files of various faculty members are far more revealing.

33. Wheeler, *Abundant Life*, 123.

34. *Ibid.*, 26.

35. Wheeler to "The President," March 17, 1903. Wheeler Papers.

36. Wheeler to Dr. Martin Kellogg, Hon. William T. Wallace, Hon. Henry S. Foote, Committee of Regents of the University of California, June 24, 1899. Wheeler Papers.

37. Arthur E. Hutson, "Faculty Government," *Centennial Record*, 290.

38. Wheeler to George Howison, July 18, 1906. Wheeler Papers.

39. Wheeler to Howison, April 2, 1908.

40. According to Wheeler's protegé, Monroe Deutsch, this criterion was still crucial after the Second World War. Deutsch does his best to spell out the qualifications of a gentleman. Deutsch, *The College from Within* (Berkeley, 1952), 58-59.

41. Fifteen years before Wheeler became president, this had been clearly stated in a remarkably frank letter from President Reid to Howison, who was considering coming to Berkeley as Mills Professor of Philosophy. The University is sometimes attacked as Godless, and the Mills Professor should try to overcome this image. An agnostic would at best have to win a place for himself. Because of mutual intolerance among churches, a sectarian would also have difficulties. But a man of "philosophic attainments, catholic views, and reverent spirit" would find a hearty welcome. The regents and public are "more liberal in their theological views than college governing boards and the public in the East usually are." Howison's experience was to bear out this assessment of the situation.

William T. Reid to Howison, January 28, 1884. Howison Papers.

42. Bowman, *Reminiscences,* 27-28.

43. Wheeler to Stephens, May 5, 1903. Stephens Papers.

44. See Clarke Chambers on Peixotto in *Notable American Women, 1807-1950,* ed. Edward T. James *et al.* (Cambridge, Mass., 1971), III, 42-43.

45. Information on Lucy Sprague (Mitchell) comes from her *Two Lives: The Story of Wesley Clair Mitchell and Myself* (New York, 1953), from Joyce Antler, *Lucy Sprague Mitchell: The Making of a Modern Woman* (New Haven, 1987); and from Gordon, *Gender.*

46. Antler, *Mitchell,* 81.

47. Lynn Gordon, writing from a modern feminist perspective, tends to approve this sort of effort for separate activities in this period, contrasting it favorably with the superficial integration that replaced it in the 1920s and 1930s.

48. Leonard Bacon, *Semi-Centennial* (New York, 1939), 27.

49. *Announcement of Courses* for 1917-18, University of California Archives. According to Frank Stricker's useful survey, the average percentage of women faculty in land-grant colleges in 1910 was 9.4. Stricker, "American Professors in the Progressive Era: Income, Aspirations, and Professionalization," *Journal of Interdisciplinary History,* XIX (1988-89): 241.

50. My statements here about minority faculty members are subject to error, since they are based on faculty names in *Announcement of Courses,* and names can be misleading.

51. Again this is spelled out by Deutsch, *College from Within,* 69. Deutsch would appoint Jews, Catholics, Japanese, even (he says with conscious daring) Negroes, provided they are "gentlemen in every sense of the term, with minds that need ask no concessions of the whites."

52. Bacon, *Semi-Centennial,* 103.

53. The grand architectural reconstruction of the campus, carried out by Howard with Wheeler's constant support and advice, is a subject outside the bounds of this study. It will be discussed at length in a forthcoming book by Sally B. Woodbridge.

54. An excellent, impartial but appreciative study of Lewis and his achievement can be found in William Jolly, *From Retorts to Lasers, The Story of Chemistry at Berkeley* (Berkeley, 1987).

55. Wheeler to George Noyes, November 3, 1919. Wheeler Papers.

56. Information about Stephens comes from his Papers, unless otherwise specified. There are helpful summaries of his life in the *Dictionary of American Biography*, and in the *University Chronicle*, XXI (1919).

57. Telegram, Wheeler and others to Stephens, January 8, 1907. Stephens Papers.

58. There is a hostile account in Bowman. It should be noted that Wheeler and Stephens forced Bowman to leave the faculty. In general Bowman speaks of the University with affection.

59. Stephens to "President Foster," November 23, 1918. Stephens Papers.

60. Stephens to Wheeler, January 26, 1912. Stephens Papers.

61. Stephens to R. J. Taussig, April 14, 1919. Stephens Papers.

62. Stephens to Wanda Becker, September 21, 1912. Stephens Papers.

63. Bowman, *Reminiscences*, 10.

64. Information about Gayley comes from his Papers; from Benjamin P. Kurtz, *Charles Mills Gayley (Berkeley 1943)* —an admiring biography by a colleague, from George R. Stewart, *The Department of English at the University of*

California on the Berkeley Campus (Berkeley, 1968), and from Bowman who contrasts Gayley favorably with Stephens, especially in his treatment of subordinates.

65. The Gayley Papers contain a great many favorable notices. He was honest enough also to preserve a fiercely hostile poem, published in the *San Francisco Examiner* of November 21, 1912, by no less a satirist than Ambrose Bierce. Bierce attacks Gayley for his anti-English prejudices (!) and also for the quality of his poetry.

66. Charles Mills Gayley, *Idols of Education* (New York, 1916), 13.

67. Bowman, *Reminiscences*, 100.

68. Gayley to Earl F. Zeisler, editor of the *Michigan Chimes*, May 19, 1925. Gayley Papers.

69. For Howison, my principal source is his Papers, which include a voluminous correspondence and also press clippings dealing with the Philosophic Forum and Bruce Kuklick, *The Rise of American Philosophy* (New Haven, 1977), which deals mainly with the "Golden Age" at Harvard. There is much information in John Wright Buckham and George Malcolm Stratton, *George Holmes Howison, Philosopher* (Berkeley, 1934), but this book by former students is impaired by undue reverence.

70. Mabel M. Lewis, *C & I* (privately printed diary, n. p., n. d. but probably written in 1966 in the author's extreme old age). This fascinating document is in the possession of Professor Bruce Kuklick, who kindly gave me a copy. (See 80n.).

71. The fullest account of this event is in John Clendenning, *The Life and Thought of Josiah Royce* (Madison, 1985), 211-20.

72. The best summary of Hilgard's career that I have seen is contained in Ann F. Scheuring, "A History of the University of California College of Agriculture," a book, soon to be published and consulted by me in typescript at the Center for

Studies in Higher Education. Hans Jenny, *E. W. Hilgard and the Birth of Modern Soil Science* (Pisa, 1961) deals briefly with Hilgard's scientific achievements and adds a few details about his Berkeley life. There is an excellent brief treatment of Hilgard's work and its significance for the University in Stadtman, *University*, 141-54.

73. Quoted by Scheuring, Chapter 2, p. 34, from a report of the Agricultural Experiment Station of 1877.

74. Bowman, *Reminiscences.* The anecdote was confirmed by Wheeler.

75. Wheeler to Lane, February 21, 1917. Wheeler Papers.

76. This episode is dealt with in Stadtman, *University*, 195-96. Wheeler's Papers mention only health as a reason for retirement.

77. Stephens to R. J. Taussig, April 14, 1919. Stephens Papers.

78. Wheeler to President H. B. Hutchins, September 8, 1920. Wheeler Papers.

79. I have discussed both these "revolutions" in my essay, "The Free Speech Movement at Berkeley: A Historian's View," in my *Ideas, Faiths, and Feelings* (New York, 1983), 87-109.

80. Perhaps one should say senior faculty. Much light is cast on the experience and feelings of junior faculty and their families by the very lively diary of Mabel Lewis, the wife of C. I. Lewis, who came to Berkeley as an instructor in philosophy in 1911 and left for Harvard, where he was to have a very distinguished career, in 1920. Mabel Lewis complains bitterly of poverty, hierarchy, and the foggy climate that she partly blames for her children's illnesses. Most of these grievances were quite real. It is also apparent that, like some other New Englanders in Berkeley in all periods, she was never able to get over homesickness for the East. Yet she also writes about the beauty of the region, the charms of San Francisco, "wonderful

evenings" of conversation and music and the supportive warmth
of her neighbors on Panoramic Way. Lewis diary (see 70n.).

81.   Salaries in 1918 were as follows:

Full professor	$3,941
Associate professor	$2,560
Assistant professor	$2,040
Instructor	$1,457

According to Stricker, "American Professors in the Progressive
Era," 240, full professors at Berkeley got less than full profes‑
sors at Stanford, about the same as those at Cornell, and more
than those at Wisconsin.

82.   Stewart, *Department of English*, 18.